Thank you
for sharing
Dear Charlotte
with me
Helen Bertrand

Dear Charlotte
by
Helen Bertrand

Library of Congress Catalog Card No. 73-92883

Jim Prewitt
Taylor Publishing Company
Dallas, Texas

ILLUSTRATIONS by FRANCES GLOVER AND CARLENE KELLY
                    (GOD BLESS THEM)
COVER DESIGN by Frances (And they both deserve more credit than this small type)

You Might Enjoy

Dedication

To: All the B's in my life

Bill
Bill, Jr.
Betty Ann
Brown Mary
And all of the beautiful
Blakeways

With Love,

B

5

A Husband With a Cold

Dear Charlotte,

And believe me, dear, there is nothing worse on God's green earth than a husband with a cold — you, yourself, can have a cold, an acute sinusitis, pneumonia, or cholera, and you will never go to bed — but a husband with a cold — that is something else.

He sneezes, he wheezes, he freezes — the house is too cold (you keep it like an icebox), the house is too hot (no wonder the bills are so high). He knows; he blows; he'll doze; he harks; he barks; he moans; he groans; he spits; he sits; he bites; he fights; he hates Kleenex; he dislikes children; he hates himself; he can't hear (ha! ha!); he can't taste; he can't smell; and in general he feels like — — — — —!

He can't take antibiotics (that's for some-one else); he can't tolerate aspirin (it upsets his bowel), and come at him with Menthola-tum, and there's a howl! Vicks Vaporub is a witch's brew, and he's forgotten that his mother could teach him a thing or two — his nose is redder than anyone's, his drip would overflow the Gulf, his cough hasn't him long for this world, and no one — absolutely no one — understands him — as he demands coffee in bed, maybe a little oatmeal with dry toast, or two coddled eggs (who's coddled?), the Houston Post, menthol cigarettes, fresh orange juice with crushed ice (beaten fine with a hammer). (I could make better use of the hammer!) He also wants a softer pillow, an extra blanket, no door bells, no dogs, no visi-tors, no children, no wife, just nobody, just leave him alone and let him die in peace —

A marvelous idea,

Just Five Words

Dean Charlotte,

With today's hemlines there is absolutely no way for a lady to bend, kneel, squat, recline, relax, dance, walk, run, stretch, yawn, climb, be dignified, or poised or charming — the lady can't by any means, SIT!

Faced with this dilemma, it dawned on me the other evening that five words from a husband to his wife have almost become extinct. How long has it been since your husband said, "Honey, your slip is showing?" These words always hinted of femininity — a bit of lace, a swish of taffeta, a peek of net, or a show of satin, silk, or embroidery.

And with the utterance of these words, knowing that he cared, you could always (in a room full of people) surreptitiously slip your hand in your neckline and yank with all your might, or pretend to straighten your suit coat as you bloused your slip over your skirt, or borrow a pin — even a straight one — and pin one strap with a prayer that you wouldn't be stabbed.

My husband recently replaced these words with five others that left me totally helpless!

I was a guest at a lovely dinner party — considered myself well-dressed in a five year old black dress (that used to be six inches longer). With the new hemline I had added long, long pearls, dark hose, and chunky, wide shoes to match my chunky, wide feet. I felt very chic and very "1969ish."

But my husband kept frowning at me across the room, inched closer and closer to me, bent down as if to give me a peck on the cheek, gave me goose pimples, and promptly erased them, as he whispered,

"Honey, your girdle is showing."

Standing,

B

The Sunday Stadium

Dear Charlotte,

My living room rug has been an Astroturf for many a Sunday; I've served popcorn and hotdogs to the spectators (two mesmerized males); and during their hypnotic state, I've feigned heart attacks, acute appendicitis, and blackouts — trying to assert my rights as a part of this family (and I use the word loosely when I say 'family'). I've talked to myself, to the dog, to the walls — but to no avail; football prevails — on Saturday, Sunday, and Monday.

Refusing to be ignored last Sunday, I tried this remark, "The course of history would have been changed had the space program chosen this date for the moon shot. There's not a man in the United States who would have gone."

Dead silence!

Trying again, "The chief concern of the 1970's seems to be the Vietnam War."

"Honey, the Chiefs and the Vikings are playing; don't you ever read the paper?" came from the oldest spectator.

As I left the stadium, I retorted, "There's a bowl of sawdust on the coffee table to munch on."

"Fine," answered one, "but it needs salt."

"Here's the salt; would you like some arsenic?"

"Sounds good; adjust the fine tuning dial before you leave."

Not easily squelched, I tried again, "The fire alarm just sounded; I think the drug store is on fire."

"Tell them to call David; he's taking calls today."

My dying attempt — "I'm leaving for the moon; maybe I'll find someone to talk to up there."

As I slammed the back door one fan yelled, "You'd better get some gas before you go; the car's empty, and pick up some ice cream on your way back!"

Slam!

B

All Sales Final

Dear Charlotte,

Ever hear of a mother disowning her child in public? I've been tempted to many times, and the temptation won last Thursday.

Betty Ann was sent to an out of town dentist for a check up, and after our appointment, we made our way to a shopping center for the 'be good' treat. I spied a particular blue shoe in a department store window, drug her into the store, deposited Bill, Jr., in the boy's department, and we sailed forth for me to try the shoes. The clerk found my size, answered my inquiry as to price (just $40.00), and slipped the right shoe on my foot. But where was the left shoe? It had disappeared — so had Betty Ann —

All of a sudden the shoe department erupted as two well-groomed ladies began a verbal fight over a blue shoe, which they had found on the summer clearance table that bore a sign reading, "All sales final — your choice $8.00." Then the clerk joined the pandemonic scene as each accused the other of putting the fall shoe on the table. My eyes searched and found my five year old under the table, calmly sucking her thumb, and watching the scene with brown-eyed amusement.

While my clerk joined the fiasco, I silently retrieved my old white shoes, quietly stole to the boy's department, bribed Bill, Jr., to go retrieve his sister, because I could hear her yelling, "I did it; I put it there; it's my Mama's shoe."

All sales final,

B

11

The Foot of a Boy

Dear Charlotte,

Have you heard the TV insurance commercial which starts, "This is the foot that kicked the skate —"? We get a bang out of it and have come up with one that fits our house.

— This is the foot of a boy who touched the floor, that walked to the hip-huggers and the paisley shirt, that skipped two steps of the stairs, that rushed to a breakfast of pancakes, that hurried to the Junior High door, that shuffled to reading and English classes, that lagged to arithmetic, that flew home for fried chicken at lunch, that left again in 10 minutes, that ran relays in PE, that slowly moved toward geography, then study hall and spelling, that dashed out of the building at 3:35, that kicked the screen door of the kitchen, that leaped toward the cabinet for a package of cookies and three jelly sandwiches, that hurried to the back yard, that kicked a football for an hour, that found six mud puddles to go through, that pedalled a bike to the drug store for a banana split, a cherry coke, and potato chips, that pumped the bicycle back to the same house, that halted in the kitchen as the question was asked, "What did you do today, honey?" — that vaulted up the stairs as the boy answered, "Nothing much; what's for supper, Mama? I'm starved!"

Love,

B

"I Slept Like a Log"

Dear Charlotte,

Oh, for the secret of sleep, which the male being possesses! The head of our household can touch a pillow or a recliner or a couch, and neither thunder, television, earthquake, nor the sounds of a sick child disturbs his slumber.

Only this morning at 4 a.m., I again marvelled and envied his ability to sleep through all sorts of disturbances. At this early hour I heard a small voice say, "Mama, come here; I'm going to be sick." Before I could reach her bedroom, blanket, sheets, pillow, pajamas, and child were ready for immediate help. I quickly transferred her to the other twin bed, and by 4:30 a.m. a feverish, nauseous little girl had unavoidably added her mark to the other bed, two floors, and a bathroom. I banged cabinet doors searching for the aspirin, dramamine, rubbing alcohol, ice bag, clean linens, fresh pajamas, carpet cleaner, dishpans, and thermometer.

I washed two loads of linens in my noisy 5 year old washing machine, made beds, scrubbed carpets, mopped and cleaned the bathrooms; and

With sick child sound asleep, I started for my bedroom, only to bump into a refreshed husband who yawned and said, "G'morning, honey, you're up early; I slept like a log; where's the paper and the coffee?" . . .DEAD SILENCE . . .

B

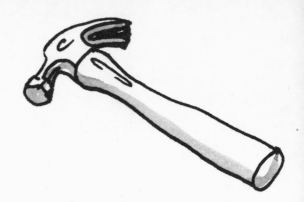

"I Hittin' It"

Dear Charlotte,

Last Wednesday morning brought a new slogan to our family — one that will be used over and over under our roof — sometimes in sincerity — sometimes with tongue in cheek. But perhaps you'd like to use it now that the lazy days of summer have been replaced with schedules, school bells, and hurry-hurry days.

Our son, who felt his importance as a high school freshman, came down the stairs the first morning of school scrubbed, combed, and polished at the early hour of 7:10; he took one look at his pajama-clad, sleepy, six year old sister and said, "Now listen, Betty Ann, you're starting to school, and you might as well know now that Mama has a rule in this house. That rule is that no one is ever late for school. So, HIT IT!"

Then came the slogan, as she swallowed a yawn with her cinnamon toast, "I hittin' it!"

Me, too,

B

My Undignified Tummy

Dear Charlotte,

Last week it was my privilege for the first time in my life to be a member of the jury panel. And tho' I fear that I shall be accused of being indelicate, I must tell you of my embarrassment.

I arose early on that Monday, so I could get the children off to school, have time to be well-groomed and arrive at the court house before 9 o'clock. But — I made one bad mistake; I skipped breakfast.

I took my seat in the court room at 8:50 and tried to look attentive, dignified, and intelligent. But my stomach had other ideas. Very loudly it began its "peristaltic perambulations" due to the loss of breakfast. Its grumblings and rumblings could have been heard at the drug store. With more than one glance directed toward me, I stared straight ahead, tried to look more dignified, and pretended that the abdominal protestations did not emit from me. As the Judge entered the courtroom, I arose with admiration and pride, and my tummy's voice — with its eggless-baconless emptiness was that of the MGM lion.

Seated, I surreptitiously fished in my purse for food, a mint, or a Life Saver — my fingers found a piece of Betty Ann's bubble gum and a Tootsie roll. Behind a Kleenex I slipped ½ of the Tootsie roll in my mouth just as the clerk began the roll call of the jury panel. With panic I tried to chew. As my name was called, I — erased of all dignity — muttered through teeth glued together, "My tummy and I are —

here!"

B

Exactly!

Dear Charlotte,

The school lunches and the mid-morning milk are wonderful benefits to our school children, but for years these benefits have turned my peaceful house into a chaotic uproar each Monday morning.

Have you ever tried to find exactly THIRTY CENTS in your house on a Monday morning at 7:45? Exactly 30 cents — not 50 — not 40! Just one quarter and one nickel, or six nickels, or three dimes, or 2 dimes and 2 nickles, or even 30 pennies!

This exact change is to eliminate bookkeeping and change-making for the teachers, and heavens knows, they need our help with 30 or more students in each class. But — somehow we never can find exactly 30 cents!

The search starts with father, as he mumbles through shaving cream, "Look on the dresser." His change consists of two pennies, a gold piece, a golf marker, a dollar bill, a ten, and a fifty (Moneybags!)

Then my handbags are turned inside out — from the new leather one to the old red straw I carried 5 years ago! Yield: a $2.00 bill, one Indian head penny, and a sixpence that I wore in my wedding shoe 20 years ago!

Betty Ann's piggy bank would yield 30 pennies, but to break the pig would cause a greater chaos than the one existing.

Bill, Jr.'s, coin collection would solve all problems, but alas, those coins are real silver, or untouched by human hands, or minted a hundred years ago.

So, as the clock ticks, I write —

"Dear Mrs. Smith, I'm so sorry to send this dollar bill (Moneybag's) to school for Betty Ann's milk. I promise it won't happen again."

'til next Monday,

B

The Mystery of Room 582

Dear Charlotte,

My friends have enjoyed my latest goof — perhaps you will. As you can see, I have called it The Mystery of Room 582.

Recently a friend of mine underwent *eye* surgery in a Houston hospital. Late one afternoon I decided to call her. Intrigued with the wonder of direct dialing, I dialed 713-526-3311 and asked for Room 582.

"Hello, my dear," I greeted her.

"Oh, how nice to hear from you," came the voice from Houston, "how are things at home?"

"Fine," I answered.

"How are your children?"

"They are well — thank heavens."

"How was your weekend?" asked the hospitalized voice.

"Just the usual chaos," I replied, "I was glad to get them back in school today. But enough of me — how are you?"

"Just great," she began, "they are going to put a pin in my right *leg* tomorrow. Dr. Brown was just here, and he says I will be walking up and down the halls in no time at all. My other leg has healed beautifully; ("LEG?" I desperately tried to say as she continued) in fact, they brought me a beautiful shiny chrome walker this morning. Can't you just see me tripping the light fantastic with that?"

"Yes," I managed to mumble — knowing full well that I was talking (or not talking) to a perfect stranger.

"Oh," continued the voice from 582, "guess what I had for lunch today?"

"I don't know," I cowardly stuttered.

"Baked custard, and it reminded me of you. I can hardly wait to get home, so you can bring me some of yours. No one makes egg custard like you."

"Thanks," I answered as I thought of my custard that always has bubbles. "Maybe I should hang up now," I gulped.

"You were sweet to call," said 582, "do give everybody at home my love."

"I will," came from bewildered me.
"Bye."

"Bye ? ? ? ? ?"

B

17

Give Me An "F"

Dear Charlotte,

Just give me an "F" in the Mama course; I didn't know the answers. Two quizzical brown eyes looked up into mine recently and asked,

"What is a white lie, Mama?"

"A white lie," I tried, "is a lie varnished by the truth."

"Uh?" came back.

"Well, a lie is a deliberate untruth, and a white lie isn't."

"What is deliberate? Does Jesus know the difference?"

"I believe He does, Betty Ann — I'm awfully busy."

"Do you ever tell a lie, Mama?"

"I try not to — it's a sin, you know."

"When you told Mary to tell Mrs. Brown that you weren't home, and you really were, was that a 'deliberate' lie or a white lie?"

"Well," I stuttered.

"And when you told Mrs. Johnson that you liked her new dress, and when she left, you said, 'That dress was terrible' — did you tell a lie or a white lie?"

"Well," came my profound reply.

"It seems to me," she continued, "that you should go to your room for a white lie. Yesterday when I said Michael hit me, and I really hit him, you sent me to my room. Why don't you have to go to your room when you tell white lies?

Does Jesus like you better than me?"

No, dear,

B

March

Dear Charlotte,

On this Sunday the Ides of March marched into our mansion as I listened to the rain on the roof and the chatter of six children (my two, plus four more).

To me March is a miserable, maddening mockery of a month. The Master must have made March to make us mindful of His many merits. He mixed His metaphors with March. He made her 31 days of mist, mystery, mildew, moisture, moans, mischief, melancholia, and migraines! March is a melodramatic misfit, who makes me think of migrating to mountains, meadows, Manila, or Manchuria.

March is mean. It makes me mean! And I mope and hope that March marches masterfully into the memorable month that precedes the masterpiece of May!

"March" ing,

B

Happy Easter

Dear Charlotte,

FOR SALE: ONE WHITE RABBIT — with pink ears, pink nose, pink eyes, and an innocent expression. He (or she) was won by a certain 8 year old at a recent Easter egg hunt. The well-meaning hostess even supplied rabbit food as she handed out white rabbits and happily said, "Happy Easter." I mumbled a greeting back to her which really meant, "Drop Dead!"

Sex of rabbit is unknown. Owner has named it Peter, but is sure it will have babies soon. Rabbit may be found under any one of six beds, or behind refrigerator, or under buffet in dining room. Rabbit may be traced by — uh — uh unmistakable signs.

Please call at 914 College between the hours of 8 a.m. and 3 p.m. while owner of rabbit is at school.

Owner was last seen between home and school wiping tears from her eyes, as Rabbit was retrieved from her school lunch box!

Please!

B

Senile

Dear Charlotte,

In the past few months I have been firmly convinced that as a mother I have completely been a failure. True, I'm not a very young parent by some standards, but I've always thought — until now — that I possessed average intelligence, good manners, and a fair amount of taste. I have even thought — until now — that I was reasonably attractive (when I work at it); my eyes aren't like Betty's or Elizabeth Taylor's, but I do have two of them; my teeth are straight, and I do have them all; and I at least try to appear well-groomed.

But now that I have a 15 year old with 15 year old friends, I feel like an extreme version of Whistler's Mother. The only acceptable thing I have done for 6 months is not wear bustles and high top shoes.

I wear the wrong color lipstick; my hair is too short and too white; my dresses are too long or too short; my hose are the wrong color; my shoes came out of Noah's Ark; I talk too loud or too soft; I even sneeze at the wrong time; in fact, I'm just blah!

After 30 years of cooking, my hamburgers, fried chicken, and peanut butter sandwiches taste just like sawdust. I drive the car too fast or too slow. I stop the car in front of or behind the stop sign; I am either hugging the curb or driving down the middle stripe. I should pass that truck or I shouldn't have passed that truck; I should have signalled for a right turn or I didn't —

These dear, bright, super-intelligent, charming fifteen year olds have me so flustered that in front of them I really don't function at all. The other day with six of them in my kitchen, I somehow managed to put the garbage in the refrigerator and the gallon of milk in the garbage can. Behind me was a dead silence and benevolent smiles, and I knew as a body they were thinking, "Poor Bill, his mother has really slipped and flipped."

The senile,

B

21

Sit a Spell

Dear Charlotte,

Know what three thought-provoking words are? — SIT A SPELL. This past Sunday morning both children were in the backyard in pajamas. It was a beautiful morning and a glorious spring world — a red bird with Monday energy, a stubborn pecan tree finally deciding to join an already green world with a new pale green dress, grass wet with April, the smell of spring better than homemade bread.

I sailed forth in high gear to fetch the Sunday paper when I heard "Sit down with us, Mama." Almost I said, "Can't — beds to make, clothes to change, bacon to fry, must hurry for Church (also read paper)," but I didn't. I decided to sit a spell.

I watched while one hit an imaginary baseball and thought how beautiful was his coordination and his world. I envied the other doing handsprings and wished that I dared.

Sit a spell — even the Bible admonishes us to sit still, stand still, be still. In this hurry-hurry world we often think that unless we are moving, life isn't what it ought to be.

We should stop and be still and cherish a Sunday morning and hold it, cherish a child and hold him, remember a neighbor who is ill, or lonely, or happy, notice a red bird and look at an April morning, sit with a friend over a cup of coffee, tell someone that you love him, and tell God that you are glad He is in His Heaven, and SIT A SPELL.

Sitting,

All is Right

Dear Charlotte,

She will be here! Don't despair! Don't give up! She was here this morning for a brief while and gone by late afternoon, but she shall return! The birds in the backyard are practicing a new choir song for her debut. The grass is desperately trying to prepare a green carpet for her. The thunder is grumbling because she hasn't arrived. The rain is trying to obliterate a whole winter of dirt, so her world will be shiny and clean. Young toes in tight shoes are squirming to be free when she comes. Bathing suits, play shorts, and baseball caps are coming out of moth balls for her arrival. Bad colds, influenza, and sinus headaches know that their days are numbered when she arrives. Hay fever, however, is lurking around the corner, and this villain awaits her. The jonquils, daffodils, and fire bushes are sporting new dresses for her entry on stage. The azaleas, wisteria, and bridal wreath are saving their costumes for her grand arrival. The wind is helping the trees with a new face lift, and their winter's complexion is being replaced. Thermometers are prepared to register a certain fever among boys and girls as she comes in. April's Fool, Easter bonnets, white shoes, straw hats, sunburn, ticks, chinch bugs, crab grass, lawn mowers, picnics, campouts, homemade ice cream, radishes and new lettuce, chiggers, and little green onions are waiting in the wings off stage — they are a part of her production.

There is just one person in the whole, wide world who refuses to applaud and cooperate, and that's the hard-headed pecan tree — it stubbornly will give no acknowledgment that she's on her way — but it will — this tree is always late for the show.

And soon SPRING will enter in all her glorious beauty, and as life begins anew, all will be right with the world.

Friday at Three

Dear Charlotte,

Oh, I can hardly wait for Friday at three
When teachers and school bells set them free.

Our summer togetherness will then begin,
And we'll visit and be visited by friends and kin.

We'll spend joyful hours together in the car,
And be asked again and again, "How far? How far?"

The days will be lazy and not hurried at all —
Oh, I just know we'll all have a ball!

Meals will be served every 30 minutes from 10 to 10
To Betty, Mike, Brad, Candy, to Bill, and to Ben.

Glasses half full of lemonade — sticky and pink
Will rest everywhere except in the sink.

A balanced diet will consist of hamburgers and hot dogs,
And no more in the mornings will they sleep like logs.

They'll be up and at 'em and ready to play,
And ask repeatedly, "Where are we going today?"

"Will you take me swimming? And please hurry, Mama;
Why are you still in your robe and pajamas?"

We'll go to the library for book after book,
And they'll be overdue without one tiny look.

I'll teach them to sew and to cook without any text.
If not this summer, then surely the next.

I'll make them assume their responsibilities, too —
Except on the days when they have something to do.

We'll burn; we'll peel; we'll be scratched and bitten,
And surely this summer I'll finish my knittin'.

After two weeks at home — you can bet your last cent,
"There's nothing to do," will be the bored lament!

As I said in the beginning, "I can't wait for Friday at three
When you, dear teachers, give them to me."

But come late August, I'll be filled with glee!
As I gladly return them, dear teachers, to thee!

What Is Liberty?

Dear Charlotte,

Our 6 year old was on her tummy, feet in the air, with a new coloring book last Tuesday evening as her father and I watched the Tuesday night movie. I looked down and said, "Why, Betty Ann, you're coloring a picture of the Statue of Liberty." — a few moments of silence and then, "Daddy, what does Liberty mean; like in the America song?"

"Well, honey, Liberty is like a bird — it means you are free —."

"But Daddy, not all birds are free; parakeets are in cages; is that Liberty?"

"That's right, dear, all birds and people aren't free."

"Why? What is Liberty?"

Daddy: "Help! Mama!"

"Liberty, Betty Ann, is being able to do as you please."

Betty Ann: "Then if I have Liberty I can eat candy for supper and not ever go to bed?"

"Well, no, Liberty must have its 'No'."

"Then it isn't Liberty if you aren't free — what is Liberty, Daddy?"

"It's going to the church that you choose; it's playing in your front yard; it's going to the school of your choice and learning; it's Christmas and birthdays, and Saturday cartoons, and quiet Sunday nights."

(From Mother, "Bravo!"),

Betty Ann: "What else is Liberty, Mama?"

"It's living in a special country — living in Jasper — it's smelling flowers, it's singing Silent Night, it's wearing a mini skirt; it's listening to a Beatle record; it's going to sleep and not being afraid, and speaking of sleep —"

"Can you buy it?"

"No."

"Can you feel it?"

"Yes, you can feel it if you have it, and really feel it if you don't have it."

"Does everybody have it?"

"No."

"Will we always have it forever and ever and live happily ever after?"

"Yes, dear, with God's help, and for your sake, we pray so . . ."

Goodnight,

B

In — and Out!!

Dear Charlotte,

Since many of my summer hours are spent in vigilance at swimming pools watching an 8 year old, who swims like a fish (and I might add, whom I could not save, ever), I decided last week that my early 1960 swim suit must be up-dated despite budget, birthdays, and bulges!

I was indeed shaken to learn that the generation gap had entered the bathing suit industry, and OH! What a GAP! If you are conservative, modest, mature — forget it! Bathing suits are bikinis, topless, strapless, backless, frontless, seamless, skirtless, see-throughs, peek-throughs, and glance-throughs, and who wants to see, peek, or glance at me? And there's not enough material in them to cover a 30 pound child — much less a 130 pound (fingers crossed) mother.

After much deliberation in the privacy of my bedroom, I rejected bathing suit after bathing suit (or they rejected me), and finally convinced myself that the one I purchased for $70.00 per yard left me with just a little dignity.

I donned my new suit, loaded the car with children, and my old terry cover-up beach robe, and headed for the swimming pool where my son was employed as a life guard. I sneaked around the corner of the building, walked quickly to the 3 foot water, dropped my robe, felt as if I were betraying all values of motherhood, and prayed to disappear as I heard a low wolf whistle from the life guard and a loud voice which said, "Boy, Mother, that bathing suit is IN!" And I whispered to myself, "Thanks, dear, it may be IN — but all of me isn't IN it!"

B

My Car? — His Car?

Dear Charlotte,

I know you have heard by now that we have another licensed driver in our house. Advantages are many — my errands are taken care of — in fact, the driver and the car have more errands than I really have. The errands take a little longer — I waited 45 minutes Sunday afternoon for hamburger buns. The Jiffy Market is a long way from our house — at least 4 blocks.

Even with permission — and we must give permission — the garage is empty, and I hope that I find a bicycle (FOR ME) under the Christmas tree.

I'm sorely afraid that some beautiful, fall Sunday morning, I shall explode! As I plopped into my (?) car this past Sunday morning, I sat on 4 slices of dill pickle, 2 containers of catsup and 6 drink straws, and my new fall suit fell! The litter basket in the front seat held French fries (cold), ½ of a cheeseburger (with onions), 6 paper cups filled with a brown Cokish water, 2 chicken legs, a melted ice cream sandwich, three apple cores, two banana peels, and my prescription sun glasses (which have rested over the sun visor for years).

In the back seat I spied 4 Coke bottles, 3 dirty white socks, a ski belt, shotgun shells, Robert's history book, Platt's Spanish textbook, one brown loafer, Janetta's baton, and a spilled bag of pop corn!

I might add, as an expensive afterthought, my gas gauge must be broken. The needle, which always pointed to "F," now sticks on the letter "E."

It is truly great to have another driver in the house.

In the house????????

Unusual?

Dear Charlotte,

How was your Mother's Day? I had a most UNusual one!

I awoke at 7:00 — put on coffee — polished a pair of disreputable brown loafers for a 16 year old — made toast — took coffee to the head of the house — shook him gently — took orange juice to a sleepy son and daughter — donned my slip, girdle, and hose — nudged Daddy again (not so gently) — yelled at the 16 year old — mended white leotards for the 8 year old — dressed her for her First Communion in an angelic white lace dress — hid the grape jelly — searched for a new razor blade for the Master of the house — cautioned the 16 year old to brush his teeth — attended Church with my family — cried happy tears for my angelic (?) First Communicant — dashed home — shed Sunday clothes — donned my apron — mixed pancakes — cut grapefruit — fried bacon — seated everyone for a late breakfast (except me) — (have never found a way to serve pancakes sitting down) — ate breakfast by myself as each excused himself — one for the paper, one for the TV, one for the playhouse — washed dishes, made beds, and picked up bathrooms — and heard, "Do a picnic, Honey, for Mother's Day — just a simple one — don't go to any trouble; Bill, Jr., and I will meet you after we play golf." Prepared picnic — met the two males — heard from one, "You forgot the butter!" — from the other — "Where's the pickle relish?" — Home from picnic — steered everyone to baths — put away picnic leftovers — cleaned up the picnic mess — put white jeans and white tennis shoes in washer to soak overnight — fed Missy dog — put out the kitchen light — headed for the shower and my bed!

An UNusual Day? Sure it was — I had a corsage! — wore it to Church — pinned it on my apron — wore it to the picnic — and before I crept into bed, I pressed it lovingly and gently between the pages of a book — the family Bible!

B

What Is a Daddy?

Dear Charlotte,

What is a Daddy?
"A Daddy is a Father on Father's Day, and after that no
one pays any attention to him."

A Daddy buys
    tricycles and bubble gum
    200 ice cream cones
    dental bills
    Christmas presents
    blue jeans and tennis shoes
    and 12 boxes of ice cream salt ('cause they're cheaper by
    the dozen)

A Daddy wears
    funny undershirts
    black shoes or brown (never red)
    white shirts and ties (except on Sunday after Church)
    one blue sock and one black one (sometimes)
    a pencil in his pocket
A Daddy looks like
    Elvis Presley
    Tom Jones
    Mr. Frank Holmes
    Uncle Jim
    Smokey the Bear (when he wakes up)
    And just like a Daddy most of the time
A Daddy doesn't
    ever play bridge
    yell like mamas do
    fix the back door

cook (except when mother brings everything outside)
ever get sick or take medicine
A Daddy looks
at television
The Houston Post
the stock market
the weather
Sports Illustrated
but never at a bird (mine doesn't)
A Daddy
works all the time
worries all the time
watches you all the time
is wonderful all the time
And a Daddy loves
Betty Ann
Bill, Jr.
drug store
golf, and
Mama

In that order,

Dear Charlotte,

The silence in our house this morning is almost unbearable. Our youngest left for her first trip without Mama and Daddy. She will be gone for three days and two very long nights. The conversation during the hour before she left went like this —

"Now, baby," her father began, "it isn't too late to change your mind. You don't really have to go."

"Bye."

"Here are some dimes and nickels for your purse in case you get thirsty."

"Bye."

Then came my parting words —

"Don't forget to brush your teeth."

"Bye."

"And remember the pink shirt goes with your pink shorts and the blue shirt goes —"

"Bye."

"Your favorite sleep toy is in the bottom of your swimming bag."

"Bye."

"And remember no swimming after you have eaten."

"Bye."

"If you want to, I am sure that you could leave the bathroom light on at night, and don't drink too many liquids."

"Bye."

"Eat all of your meat and not just French fries. Keep up with your clothes, especially your shoes; be sure there are two."

"Bye."

"Remember all of your name, our street, and our telephone number. Mind your manners, say your prayers, and be a sweet girl."

"Bye."

Bye, dear

B

What If?

Dear Charlotte,

I know a very masculine man who can cope with almost anything — he can hit a beautiful golf shot, long, straight and to its point; he can outswim his 16 year old son and was known as Wisconsin's youngest life saver at the age of 9 when he rescued a two year old child; he lost his teeth playing high school football and once ran 95 yards for a touchdown; he was a baseball catcher and a good one; he mastered water skis on the first try only a month ago; he won a medal with ski jumping in the snow; he can beat many a person at a game of pool; is a better than average bridge player — masters almost anything — would defend his Church, his home, his country, his community, his business with his life; went back to school after World War II and made good grades in physics, chemistry, and economics — but oh, there is one thing with which he can't cope — A CHIGGER!

This tiny, minute, diminutive creature or bug or thing sends him into orbit — he screams; he yells; he whelps; he swells; he scratches; he claws; he gnaws; he growls; he howls; he cusses; he fusses; he can't sleep (or anyone else); he cries; he sighs; he surrenders, and one little, bitty bug robs him of all his glory —

What if a Chigger were bigger?

Love,

B

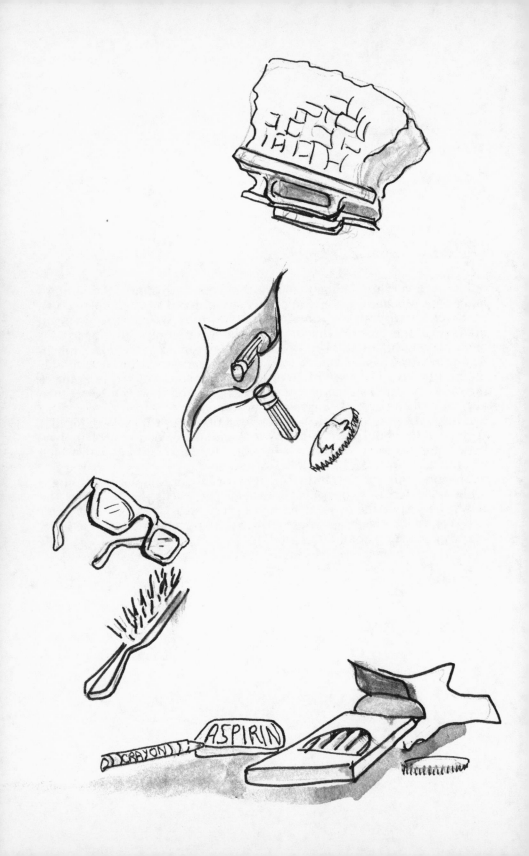

Please, Just One Quarter

Dear Charlotte,

How you would have chuckled had you had a birds-eye view of me last Thursday afternoon. You and B. J. both will say, "It could only happen to her!"

My daughter and I drove into the St. Elizabeth's Hospital entrance only to be barred from the parking lot by a yellow and black arm-like gate. And this gate opened only with the insertion of a quarter in the slot of a meter within arm's reach of my right window.

I opened my old navy bag, quickly found my change purse, which yielded 32 pennies, a St. Christopher medal, one dime, a baby tooth, 10 S & H green stamps, one half dollar, two gold safety pins, and one nickel! Totally undaunted, I began to fish for change in my bag. Out came glasses, note pad, pencils, kleenex, letters, hair brush, makeup, and twenty other unrelated items. My fingers touched another half dollar, and then —

Horns from ten cars backed up on busy Calder Street began to sound, and with a frantic glance in my rear view mirror, I realized that this angry bevy of noise was directed at me!

"Mama, hurry, hurry!" came from my companion. "Those cars are getting mad at you."

Another desperate search produced 3 pennies and an English sixpence!

Just as I reached the point of tears, a gallant, exasperated member of the superior sex slammed the door of his car, stomped toward mine, and with hand outstretched, he handed me a beautiful, shiny, United States of America QUARTER!

I smiled my most charming Sunday smile, and stammered, "Bless you!"

"Never mind the blessings or the quarter," he bellowed, "Move, lady; just MOVE!"

Thanks,

B

Communicating

Dear Charlotte,

My son and I are most uncommunicative — we don't talk — in the early morning hours — those of you who do — God bless you!

But I must have at least three cups of coffee before I can attempt any sensible conversation. And my almost-adult child must consume a minimum of three pieces of toast and a king size Coke before he wakes up — completely. Over all of his school years, we managed three words each morning — the usual "Good Morning" from me, and "Mornin'" has been his answer. These words have been the quotient of our communication for the past twelve years before noon. We both enjoy each other's silence and appreciate the other's thoughtfulness — we do not invade the other's privacy; and we understand each other in our non-verbal communication.

But this morning our conversation lengthened — not by more than three or four words — but oh, the joy and meaning of those words! I had begun the day as droopy as a rain-soaked crepe myrtle, and suddenly my heart soared, and my day kaleidoscoped into rosy hues.

I was on my way to Beaumont at the early hour of 6:30, and Bill, Jr., was on his way to a summer job, but we had 15 minutes of silence to share. We had exchanged our "good mornings," and as I opened the back door, I said "G'bye, dear," — "Bye," he managed. And then came from my son my very own parental entreaty used so many times through the years,

"Be careful, Mama."

Communicating,

B

Packing

Dear Charlotte,

Our daughter's foot locker is all packed and ready for camp. Along with the inventory of her clothing, I have pasted this note inside the trunk lid:

To Whom It May Concern:

This is a very special little nine year old girl. She is especially special with her father, and he isn't quite sold on this trip to camp. However, if you know a few important things about her, I am convinced she'll be the camper of the year.

She likes coffee milk brought to her bed each morning; that's just a little coffee in a cup of milk with lots of sugar. She doesn't eat breakfast early, but about ten o'clock she likes soft scrambled eggs, bacon (crisp), and toast (cinnamon, please). She doesn't like spinach, carrots, roast beef, ham, cabbage, green peas, beets, sausage, oatmeal, and milk. But she loves ice cream (vanilla), soup (chicken noodle), hot dogs (with mayonnaise), hamburgers (with catsup), French fries, Cokes and candy!

She has never spent the night away from home except with her grandparents and a few special friends. And she may wake up at three o'clock in the morning with a horrible stomach ache and want to come home. Oh, incidentally, we always leave the bathroom light on for her at night — she doesn't like the dark. And I should tell you she doesn't like lightning and thunder, and she always crawls into bed with us on a stormy night. She also kicks her covers; so, if you are up at two a.m., please check on her; she might get cold.

She doesn't like to brush her teeth or her hair, but if you will patiently remind her about six times each morning, she will cooperate.

She doesn't like to go to bed on a summer night, but if you will let her watch just a portion of the 10 o'clock movie, this will solve the bedtime problem, especially if you give her a glass of orange juice and cookies after you have kissed her goodnight three times.

If you will remember these few likes and dislikes of our child, I'm sure she will love camp. But if she doesn't, we will appreciate your calling 384-2525, or 384-2626, or 384-3649, or 384-3240, or 384-4548, or 271-2249. Anyone of these people will be happy to pick her up —

B

P.S. Please don't change her; we like her just the way she is.

Unpacking

Dear Charlotte,

When a mother UNpacks a little girl's foot locker from camp, she finds:

  1 musty, smelly, dirty, mildewed trunk
  1 bar of Ivory soap with the wrapper intact (30 days without soap?!?!?!?)
  1 tube of unsqueezed Crest, complete with cap?!?!?!
  6 black and grey towels, which once were a lovely pink
  6 shirts out of a possible 12, two with mildew, 2 which aren't hers, one with PEACE scrawled on the front, one with DROP DEAD written on the back
  3 FIRST prize blue ribbons — one for the softball throw — one for the football kick — one for the girl's relay and one white ribbon for a third place in the 100 yard dash — not bad — how she'll hate me for saving them when she's 16!
 24 eight cent stamps — all stuck together — no wonder she sent an SOS for postage
10 postcards, which read "Dear Mother" and were never mailed
  7 letters from me to her just like the Ivory soap — UNOPENED!
  2 pair of lovely nylon pajamas, slightly damp, never worn, in the bottom of the trunk
  1 bottle of Merthiolate — open
 ½ of a bathing suit
  2 Butterfingers (go-o-o-e-y)
10 pair of underwear all neatly folded, as I remembered folding them
  4 Church bulletins — God bless her!
  1 pass to the infirmary for undetermined injuries?!?!?!?!
  1 merit for Neatness and Cleanliness?!?!?!?

And finally, may I add that the mother who happily brought the little girl home with her foot locker found her daughter slimmer, taller, older, and wiser — oh, that the mother were —

                                 Wiser,

Someone Goofed

Dear Charlotte,

Just read the section of our paper on organized baseball for our children, and it brought back many a memory — mostly memories with tears — tears brought on by adults.

Sure, we wanted our son to play farm league, little league, and Babe Ruth league — I say "We" — at least his father was quite sure that he was a natural and would field, catch, pitch, and hit! What a dream!

I can still remember him with his blonde hair (crew cut) as a little boy as he proudly took his turn in center field — after some 4 or 5 innings, he became bored, found him a stick, knelt down on his knees and began to draw pictures in the dirt, and, of course, you've already guessed. The ball sailed over his head and over the fence, as his father agonized and the adult stands turned my blood to ice water with, "Who is that stupid kid in center field?"

And another evening when his team had lost 16 to 4 and at long last I had him in the back seat of the car, crying his little heart out, I said, "Honey, it's not whether you've won or lost, but how you played the game," and he sobbed, "Mother, how can I play the game when I never got off the bench?"

And the darkest of all his career was a little league ballgame with the score tied 9 to 9 with the bases loaded, in the last of the ninth with two outs, and he was called off the bench as a pinch hitter — and the count went — S-T-R-I-I-I-K-E, Ball one (as I prayed, "please hit it, honey"), S-T-R-I-I-I-K-K-E TWO ("STUPID UMPIRE!!!! Please dear God, just one time let him be a hero.") — and then it came — STRIKE THREE, AND YOU'RE OUT!"

And then his heart-breaking words at home, "Well, Daddy, everyone said I lost the ballgame; I sure goofed, didn't I?"

B

P.S. No, dear, *you* didn't goof!

Does God Wear Glasses?

Dear Charlotte,

Do you suppose God wears glasses?

When I was a child and a young adult, I was disciplined or admired by an adored and adoring Dad, who merely gave me a glance over his glasses. If he approved of me, the eyes over the glasses carried a twinkle; if he disapproved of my behavior, the twinkle was replaced with something that said to me, "Behave, or else!" I never needed the else — that look over those glasses did the trick. Even this Christmas as he was our welcomed guest and one of the children answered 'Yeah' to him, I received the glance over the glasses which said, "You need the spanking; teach them better."

But back to my Heavenly Father. As I sat in Church Sunday, trying hard to concentrate on the sermon and my prayers, I know that God was looking over his glasses at me — my thoughts were —

"Our Father Who art in Heaven" — (Oh, good *heavens,* Betty Ann is making an airplane out of the bulletin — please, please don't let her fly it.)

"Hallowed be Thy name" — (What's the *name* of that woman in the front row in that beautiful blue hat?)

"Thy kingdom come, Thy will be done" — (*done!* oh, my goodness, did I turn the oven off? Bill likes the roast rare — not done.)

"On earth as it is in Heaven" — (*Earth* — Bill, Jr., has enough dirt in his ears to plant a garden — *heaven* — there goes Betty Ann's bulletin airplane — please, let it go to Heaven and not to the altar.)

"Give us this day our daily bread" — (I forgot to take the rolls out of the freezer — toasted hamburger buns with overdone roast — what a Sunday dinner!)

"And forgive us our trespasses" — (I'd look pious in that blue hat; it must have cost $35.00, and it doesn't do one thing for her.)

"As we forgive those who trespass against us" — (Why doesn't that mother do something with that child that is kicking the seat behind me? I just can't pray with that distraction!)

"And lead us not into temptation" — (Some of these days when Bill, Sr., punches me in the ribs and glares at the children as if he knew them not — I'm going to punch him right in the nose.)

"But deliver us from evil" — (Oh my, the sermon is over, and I haven't even finished the Lord's Prayer.)

If God wears glasses (and he must with all the looking He has done from so far away for so many years; (wonder if he's far-sighted or near-sighted), then I know He is looking over them and saying, "Helen, behave, or else!"

No twinkle for me,

Nothing to Do????

Dear Charlotte,

Men surely are funny creatures. They are convinced that women do nothing all day long.

My list of things to do to get ready for vacation read like this — take car to garage for checkup, have wheels aligned, have it washed and greased, check credit cards, buy Daddy pair of sun glasses, ask filling station for road map, pick up thermos bottle at drug store, fill it with coffee for the driver, buy plastic cups, check small ice box, fill with soft drinks, cheese, fruit, buy car sickness pills, allergy pills, pick up film, fill camera, be sure shoes are shined, buy two games for children to play in car, take paper, pencils, crayolas, ask Scott to buy bacon and eggs and place in ice box, also ask him to water the yard and house plants, also ask him to pick up paper and mail, ask the neighbor to turn on the air conditioner in two weeks, remember to turn it off, change the beds, pay bills, place bread, milk and hamburger fixings in freezer for return supper, be sure that all clothes are clean and packed in four bags — being sure to pack a "take out" bag for overnight stay at motel, don't forget bathing suits, golf clubs, and skis, pack zippered bag for hanging clothes, being sure that Daddy's are on top, check to be sure haircuts and shampoos are done, make sandwiches for lunch in car (how I'd love to go somewhere and not have to eat in the car), pack car, being sure everything is neat and in place (Daddy hates anything loose), take the dog and its food to the neighbors, also gold fish and food — pick up Daddy at drug store and hear him say,

"Well, we made it; your hair needs combing, Mama; what have you been doing?"

Nothing, dear,

B

S-h-u-t t-h-e D-o-o-r

Dear Charlotte,

At the end of this long summer's day I am sitting in the backyard and looking up at the brassy July sky and wondering if Heaven is air conditioned and who pays the bills and if there are back doors up there. If God has air-conditioning and back doors, he just couldn't remain patient, kind, and good. For at least six hours of the day, I have closed each conversation with these words —

It all began this morning when Betty Ann and Mike decided to build a tree house —

Enter back door — "Mama, Mike and I need the hammer; where is it?" (In the hall closet — please, close the back door).

5 minutes later — "I'm thirsty, can I have a drink of water?" (May I? Mike. And please shut the door).

3 minutes later — "We don't have any nails, Mama — do you got any?" (Have, not got — shut that door!).

Mike again — "Where's the ladder, and do you have a saw?" (In the garage, Mike, and the door, please, M-I-I-I-C-H-E-E-A-L).

2 minutes later — "I've got to go to the bathroom, and could we have some cheese and crackers, Mom, and make us some Coolaid?" — (No, it will soon be lunch — P-L-L-E-E-A-S-E remember the door).

2 seconds later from the OPEN back door — "Lunch? What's for lunch? — oh, no, not chicken again; can Mike eat with us? (Yes, and please S-H-U-T T-H-E D-O-O-O-R-R!!!).

And on and on and on until — "We're hot, Mama, do you have an extension cord, and where is the fan; the cord has to be a long one to reach to the top of the tree — (No, dear, AND B-E-E-T-T-T-Y A-A-A-N-N-N, will you CLOSE THE DOOR????).

Just a blessed 15 minutes and then, "Mike won't play right, and I'm not going to bring all that stuff in by myself — will you help me?" (Yes, X!??!X&! it, and WILL You P-l-e-e-e-e-a-se SHUT T-H-A-A-A-T DOOR!!!!).

On second thought — there is probably no July in Heaven! There are just Aprils and Mays and no air conditioning and no Mamas who are impatient —

And that excludes,

B

What's for Dinner?

Dear Charlotte,

Men (in particular one) make me sick (er) sometimes!

Early yesterday I awoke with a new, unnamed virus that made my tummy feel as if it had been hit by the University of Texas defensive line. I flew to the nearest bathroom and resided therein most of the day.

My nausea had reached its peak when my husband arrived home at noon to keep his Wednesday afternoon golf game, and neither rain, sleet, snow, nor a dying, bathroom-ridden wife interferes with this weekly addiction.

His unsympathetic voice had lost its euphonic lilt as he fired these questions: "Why didn't you go to the doctor? What have you taken? Do you have any fever? Where's my green golf cap? (GREEN?????) You don't have any real symptoms, do you? Why are you still wearing your robe? What's for lunch? Why isn't the bed made? I'm sure you won't mind if I play golf, will you?"

"No," I managed weakly from the depths of the lavatory with these thoughts: IF I die, I pray that you'll be on number 17 tee, two under par, right in the middle of your back swing when they give you the message that I'm gone! (And even then I'm sure that you would finish your game and verify the message from Number 19).

Just for spite, however, I somehow survived the afternoon, but disdained all thought of food and dinner for my devoted husband. And you already know that Would-Be-Arnold Palmer returned with concern, verbally replayed his 18 holes, and then asked, "What's for dinner?"

My stomach and I suggested oatmeal, dry toast, scrambled eggs, or potato soup. But, in his usual unselfish way, he said, "I know you don't feel well, honey, but I'm starved; just boil some shrimp, and I'll help peel them. If you'll grind the garlic in the olive oil, I'll make the salad, and for dessert I'll have some of that mince pie with rum sauce if you'll warm the sauce and add just a little more rum." . . .

OH-H-H-h-h-h-h-h-h-h-h-h-h!!!

B

46

E-n-t-h-u-s-i-a-s-m

Dear Charlotte,

Do you greet each day with enthusiasm? It is one of the secrets of success. Through the stimulus of a Self-Improvement course, the reading of Benjamin Franklin's life, and the prodding of some early-rising, wide-awake friends (?), I decided last week that my whole life would be more beautiful if I greeted each morning with enthusiasm at six o'clock, instead of my usual hour of 7:15.

My first (and only) new-scheduled day began as I groped in the darkness for the jarring jangle of the alarm clock. I jumped from my deliciously warm bed, straddled the leg of the bed with two toes, muttered an unlady-like word, and heard a sleepy husband ask, "What's the matter; where you goin'?"

"Nothing's wrong; I'm being enthusiastic," I yawned, "and I've just broken my little toe."

"Well, be a little quieter with your enthusiasm," came the comforting, sympathetic reply from the depths of a pillow.

Missy, the bulldog, who usually follows me to the kitchen at 7:15 with an enthusiastic wag of her tail, opened one quizzical eye and immediately closed it — (smart dog — smarter than some people).

A part of my enthusiastic improvement program was that I should discard my old blue robe and sloppy houseshoes and be fully clothed and well-groomed at this hour . . . (Ugh!) In my sleep I became a fashion plate in red tennis shoes, black slacks, and a brown shirt. I flipped on lights to apply my face and gave up when I stuck a mascara brush into one sleepy eye. Next, I plugged in the coffee, made the usual four pieces of toast, and sat enthusiastically.

When my daughter came into the kitchen at 7:15, I had drunk a whole pot of coffee and eaten all the toast. She looked at me and said, "Did you sleep in your clothes, Mama? You don't match, and where is my toast?"

My son came down the stairs at 7:45, glanced at me, and said, "Where'd you get that black eye, Mother? You sure look sleepy; why don't you go back to bed?"

A great idea — all alone at 8:15, I slipped back into my bed with the morning paper, with a case of coffee nerves, and with

Enthusiasm,

B

Size Eight and a Half

Dear Charlotte,

Dreaming (not believing) that I could look like Iris, Carolyn, or Kathryn (despite our age difference — and that's not the only difference), I bravely walked into the shoe salon of a big department store and said, "I'd like to see some black boots." "What size, MISS?" the chic clerk chirped. "Size eight and a half," I whispered so no one could hear. (Did she say Miss? — oh, brother!) I pushed my feet into what looked like two wrinkled black pontoons. My beautiful saleslady purred, "Darling, these are truly high fashion." (Yes, high enough to make my knees look like balloons and also high enough to wreck a week's budget.) "They will be a major item in your spring wardrobe," she tried again. (Major, I mused, I look just like a fat 50 year old drum major.) "This patent wears well and is so easily cleaned," the sales pitch continued. (Patton, if I had a helmet with five stars and held a riding crop, I'd look like General Patton.)

Three familiar faces seemed to peer at me from the sea of mirrors, and I could hear them say —

"Oh, Mother, you bought some boots. Is it gonna snow? They sure are big, and you sure look funny."

"Honey, those boots remind me of our courting days when you wore a size 8 dress, and you looked great in gaberdine jodphurs and your riding boots, remember?"

"Gee, Mother, those would be great for duck hunting, and you wouldn't have to worry about snakes."

As I slipped my left foot with its corn back into my tired I. Millers, I said to the clerk, "Thank you, these aren't exactly what I had in mind. I would like to look around. I may be back later."

"Yes, MADAM!"

B

49

Slumber????????

Dear Charlotte,

There is an American institution called a slumber party. I'm sure it is American, because only we could so misuse a word. My dictionary says — "slumber means to sleep; to be in a state of rest (rest??); to be inactive" (INACTIVE?!?!) — oh, what a misnomer when we use the word 'slumber' to describe a certain kind of a party.

I'll prove it. Take (please, take them) 6 jiggling, giggling, wiggling little 9 year old girls, add six assorted sleeping bags, 6 pillows of all sizes, 2 tote bags, 2 overnight bags, 1 paper sack, and 1 Mama's makeup case filled with pajamas of all descriptions, 5 tooth brushes (1 missing), Barbee dolls, crayolas, two record players with records, bubble gum, school books, and six changes of clothing for morrow (which will be a long time coming). Place them and these in your family room (they or these won't stay there), but begin there! Be sure that your kitchen holds at least 24 Cokes, weiners, mayonnaise, buns, potato chips, peanut butter, cough syrup, popcorn, cookies, Kleenex, band aids, doughnuts, orange juice, and aspirin (for yourself!).

Now, you are ready for a slumber party, and you can retire (another misnomer) to your room and relinquish all rights to the peace and privacy of your home.

At midnight when you have zippered all sleeping bags (and mouths), permitted last drinks of water, suggested visits to the bathroom, found two lost pillows, and tiptoed through potato chips and popcorn to your own bed (where father is snoring), don't believe for one minute that Morpheus has six little girls in his arms — just wait —

During the next five hours stay mobile, Mama, 'cause you'll hear:

"Mama, come quick; Susie just vomited all over her sleeping bag and Mary's pillow" —

An hour later — "Mama, wake up, Diane wants to go home; she lives out in the country, can we all go with you to take her?"

30 minutes later — "Mary and I are cold; can we sleep in my bed?"

4:00 a.m. — "Mama, Susie needs some dry pajamas; she says that someone spilled some water on her sheet."

5:00 a.m. — "Mama, wake up; Ann is scared, 'cause they told ghost stories; can we sleep with you and Daddy, Mama?" —

6:00 a.m. — "We don't want doughnuts for breakfast; Ann wants oatmeal; I want scrambled eggs, and Diane hates eggs — are you awake, Mama?"

Slumbering,

B

Togetherness

Dear Charlotte,

Summer togetherness doesn't happen very often these days with a 19 year old and an eleven year old — miles apart — one prefers the Top Burger and one loves the swimming pool. But this past Sunday afternoon around four o'clock, my almost-man son said with a little boy's nostalgia, "Mother, let's make some homemade ice cream." And happiness pervaded our house as everyone awoke and demanded center stage.

"OK," I said, "If you will go get some ice." and the TOGETHERNESS began —

"I want strawberry like you get at the Carnation Place," came from the youngest.

"No," came from the oldest, "we're going to make banana nut."

"No bananas," came from me, "and nuts are too high."

From the depths of the television set came the Master's voice, "Vanilla — the boiled custard kind like my mother used to make; you have the recipe." (Leave it to him to complicate matters — his mother's recipe takes one hour of stirring — and after 30 years of cooking I still hear that "my mother" bit!)

As I longed for Pistacio Nut, the Baskin Robbins' kind, I began to scald milk, beat eggs, and measure the sugar — you know who had won again!

I reminisced with the children and recalled that as a small child we didn't have electric freezers and that I had to sit on the freezer as my Dad turned and turned, and that he admonished me to "sit hard" or the ice cream wouldn't freeze, and being a dutiful child to an adored parent, I would try so desperately to sit hard. "Bet you had a cold seat," came from my daughter. "If you had to do all that work; why not buy ice cream?" came from the teenager.

Not a bad idea, I thought, as I looked in the ice box freezer and found vanilla, strawberry, banana nut, no pistacio —

But, remember there is no togetherness in an ice box.

B

It's 10 O'clock

Dear Charlotte,

"It's 10 o'clock, do you know where your children are?"

"These familiar, thought-provoking words are heard by most of us each night from Channel 4 TV. What are your reactions to this question? I have often felt smug, reassured, grateful, thankful, and blessed. I have answered in my heart and audibly, "Yes, I do — this night, this week, this month, this year." I pray that I can always say "Yes" — especially when I remember the events of the past week, the years of war, traffic statistics, juvenile problems.

However, with the gift ???? of daylight saving and the end of the school year, my reaction has been one of irritation. When I hear, "Do you know where your children are?" I want to snap, "I surely do, because I know where they've been.""

Evidence in the kitchen: freezer door open, ice trays empty, 6 dirty glasses on the drain, remnants of 4 peanut butter sandwiches (after dinner), tops off of jelly and peanut butter jars, 3 cabinet doors open, 2½ pairs of tennis shoes (always one missing), 5 socks (ditto). Evidence in bathroom: 2 faucets steadily dripping, 4 wet towels for 2 children, water-filled bathtub with 6 bath cloths and 3 floating bars of soap, discarded clothing on the floor, two tubes of toothpaste without caps. Evidence in the hall: 2 chlorine soaked bathing suits, one baseball glove, 2 Barbee dolls, half-eaten apple on the stairs, an empty potato chip sack, a puddle of red, unidentifiable goo on the carpet, and a frog in a jar! Same give-away, tell-tale signs in bedroom: dirty shirts, broken crayons, Post Toasties, scattered toys, unopened books, a blaring television, a record player that won't hush, and overnight little guests that have insomnia . . .

Yes, I know where my children are — very much at home.

Gratefully,

B

Little Mountains

Dear Charlotte,

Little mountains sometimes are the very hardest to climb. We, as parents, try to teach our children how to climb the tallest ones — the heights of happiness, success, and faith. But, oh, we overlook those little hills that can become a Mount Everest!

This came home to us this past Sunday as we prepared our ten year old for a year at boarding school. With our hearts bursting with love, misgivings, doubts, fears, and hope, we encouraged with —

"You will have a wonderful time, honey; you will meet new friends; you will live in a great big dormitory with other little girls; you will always have someone to 'spend the night'; you will have a house mother; it will be just like college . . ."

"I know, Mama, but I can't make my bed very good."

"And you'll have all sorts of new activities; you can go swimming every day; you will learn to play tennis; there are ballet classes at school; you will love the PE program, and you will be taken to your own church each Sunday . . ."

"But I can't make the sheets very smooth."

"You will learn your numbers; those hard words will soon be easy to sound; by mid-term you will find your science and geography much easier; and your room mother will help you with your homework."

"Yes, Mama, how do you get the bedspread under the pillow? I can never make it fold under right."

"Before you know it, it will be Thanksgiving and you'll be home, and then it will be Christmas, and then your Easter holidays, and summer will be back, and you will . . ."

"Mama, you won't listen — I'll never get my bed made; you never would let me, 'cause I couldn't get the bumps out."

Little mountains,

B

The More the Merrier

Dear Charlotte,

Sometimes I think a mother should take her bath at 4 a.m. or buy stock in a deodorant company and forget her daily bath.

Last Friday afternoon at 5:45 — almost two hours before game time — I decided to pamper myself with a hot, leisurely bath. Not a single child was in sight — all gone or playing next door.

No sooner was the water running than . . .

A frantic knock on the door, and "Mother —," "I can't hear you;" I yelled, "I'll be out in a minute."

"What's for supper?" yelled back, "I'm starved."

"I'll be out in a minute — wait."

"I can't. I'll be late for the game."

"You have two hours — look in the oven."

— Nothing like a leisurely bath —

As Betty Ann, who doesn't believe in knocking, bursts through the door, leaves it open, and breathlessly says,

"Mama, the yard man is in the kitchen and wants to see you, can he? And can Lisa spend the night?"

"May . . . not can . . . and the answer is No and Yes in that order . . . WAIT A MIN- UTE!!"

The hungry one is back with a knock, "Mother, I need the medicine for burns; the oven was hot!"

Betty Ann again, "Mother, Michael has to use the bathroom. Can he come in?"

"No!!!!"

A yell from the kitchen, "Mother, Daddy wants you on the telephone, and he says it is important."

Dripping across three rooms to a refuge of privacy — "Yes, dear?"

"Honey, the plumber is coming to fix the leaky faucet in the back bathroom."

"Send him right up, dear; the more the merrier!"

"??????"

B

Just the Two of Us

Dear Charlotte,

Ever dream of just what you and your husband would do when your children were gone, and at last you were alone? I've had such dreams, and they were visions of quiet, romantic evenings together, recapturing the beautiful glow of early marriage. Our conversations would be scintillating and uninterrupted; we would take long week-end trips — just the two of us — without a guilty conscience for leaving the children at home with a sitter — our car would be filled with taped music instead of kids, dogs, candy, backseat fights, color books, and tuna fish sandwiches; we could finish all sorts of unfinished projects together; we could read all of those books collected during the years; we would enjoy a new togetherness with no confusion, noise, nor schedule — we would be free.

My dreams haven't come true; have yours? We spend endless hours staring into space, or glaring at each other — each one seeming to say, "It's all your fault." We are both super sensitive with our feelings — easily ruffled; we run over each other getting to the mail box and the telephone; we both seem to be searching for something, and it isn't each other. For the first time in our busy, happy lives, we are like the children, there is NOTHING to do.

We have both recalled a telephone conversation with our dear friends, Thos and Marion, when a few years ago their Pat and Karen had gone away to school. To the question, "What are you doing?" came the exciting reply from Thos, "What are we doing, dear? — well, we're sitting here eating a peach."

Dreaming,

B

P.S. I'm searching for a bushel of peaches.

Hurry!

Dear Charlotte,

"Poems are made by fools like me! but . . ."

There is a fashion show going on just north of Jasper on Highway 96 — it is best seen from your car window on a sunny afternoon about four o'clock. The colorful costumes could not be created by Dior or any fashion designer. The admission charge is a heart full of appreciation.

You must drive to Rayburn Country, make the circle in the village, return on the same highway. The ladies of the forest are screaming for applause in their leafy gowns of grapefruit yellow, metal bronze, pumpkin orange, maroon, apple reds, persimmon pink — all the trees are parading their fall fashions — except the pine trees, who are green with envy. But the pines are whispering in ladylike fashion, "Just wait, in two weeks their dresses will be gone — they'll be grey and bare. Then people will look at us and say, 'What a lovely Christmas tree.' "

Go see the fashion parade, but HURRY before the show closes, The Designer and Producer must join the celebration of His birthday!

"Only God can make a tree!"

B

The Time Will Come

Dear Charlotte,

If you ever wish that your children weren't under your feet all day long, and if you have ever longed for another name except "Mama" (and God knows that any Mother at sometime has had such thoughts), just know that time will take care of this, and your wish will come true.

Then the bedrooms will be neat and clean; there won't be any bumps in the linens — they will be straight, smooth, and empty; there will be potato chips in the pantry, unopened Cokes in the ice box, an abundance of vanilla ice cream, and black bananas in the fruit bowl. You won't have to get up at four a.m. to pull a cover, give assurance after a nightmare, touch a feverish forehead, hunt the thermometer, or spill purple cough syrup on the blanket. You can sleep all night and not listen. And if you do listen, you will hear nothing but silence.

You can look at the pennants on the wall, the football ribbons on the bulletin board, the kindergarten diplomas, the junior high report cards, the program for a high school graduation — and you can listen to the silent tape player, the voiceless radio, and the telephone that doesn't ring. You won't even have to burn the back porch light — no one is coming in. You won't have to bake an apple pie or pick up shoes in the hall or find a lost Barbee doll under the couch or put the lid on a jar of grape jelly or fry hamburgers at nine p.m.

You can have your beautiful privacy — you can read the paper; you can drink your coffee; you can find your toothbrush and your comb; you won't need a baby sitter; you won't need anything — EXCEPT THEM — they are out from under your feet — and you are at last

Free and lonely,

B

A Pair of Grey Hose

Dear Charlotte,

I heard a fashion expert say the other day that your hose should match your hemline — with my knees that blouse and my legs that should have been four, I'm glad that I don't have a purple dress.

Remember during World War II that you were blessed if you possessed one pair of nylons, and if you did own these treasures, you wore them 'til they were faded? You then tinted them with Rit and wore them proudly with red, navy, grey, black, white, or pea green dresses.

These memories came back to me recently as I dashed into a large department store in a city and said, "I've ruined my hose, I want a pair of grey hose — size 10½."

A stone-faced clerk, who looked as if she had stepped out of Vogue and acted as if she owned Humble Oil and was selling hose for a lark, stuck her lovely, well-powdered nose in the air and said,

"We have hundreds of pairs of grey hose. Do you want Seams? Seamless? Mesh? Textured? Sheer? Opaque? Short? Medium? Long? Nude? Colored? Light? Dark? Flesh? Support? Panty? Bikini? Glitter? Wet look? Ankle high? Knee high? Waist high? Thigh high? Body? Orthopedic???"

Wishing that I could afford to reply, "I'll take six pairs of each and deliver them to my penthouse within the next 30 minutes," I put my shiny, sunburned, not-so-classic nose a foot higher than the clerk's and pretended that I had one oil well, and said,

"If it is all right with you, I want a pair of grey hose, size 10½."

Aging,

B

He Is Gone

Dear Charlotte,

He is gone —
Maybe he won't be President of the United States (and I was sure that he would be), or a surgeon, or a pharmacist (his father was sure on this score), or a scientist, or a Bobby Layne (another wish from his Dad) — but,
He will be missed by his two parents, who have been grateful for his footsteps in an upstairs bedroom, and suffered the endurance of a radio, a tape player, and a TV — all turned on at the same time.
This past week I kept forgetting that he was a very important, all-knowing college freshman, and I goofed with, "Honey, be sure to pack this"; "Have you done so and so?"; "Don't forget to do this"; and his patient answer to all was, "Mother, I'm 19; I'm grownup and not a two year old!"
He departed yesterday with a car bursting with tapes, records, clothes, golf clubs, his father's check book, my Enco card, 2 dozen tuna sandwiches, a head of long hair, and a car with two mufflers which awoke the cemetery!

And he left at home —
  His toothbrush
  His fountain pen
  His notebook
  His class schedule
  His shaving kit
  His sheets and pillow cases
  His soap
  His deodorant
  His socks
  His Mother
  His Father

And a quiet, quiet house with 19 years of memories —

B

He Is Back

Dear Charlotte,

He is back!
   Our college freshman, who had proclaimed to the world that he might not be home 'til Thanksgiving, drove into the driveway last Friday afternoon after 5 days of college, and he brought with him —

   4 loads of dirty clothes
   The bravado of a lion
   The knowledge of a PhD.
   The insecurity of a lamb
   The fear of a first grader
   $70.00 worth of brand new books with such
   formidable titles as Chemical Calculations, Trigo-
   nometry, College Algebra, and Engineering Drawing
   1 slightly used credit card
   An explanation for three collect telephone calls
   A check book minus a few checks
   And a car that needed repair
   One profound statement, "Mother, you'll just never
   believe the price of groceries!"

   And the question for which I had been waiting, "What's to eat, Mother; I'm starved?"
And a grin that said, "It's good to be home."
Also, a reluctance to leave the house (which didn't exist a few days ago),
And a hundred boy noises which brought the house back to normal.

   It wasn't Thanksgiving, but it was

B

"Wither Thou Goest"

Dear Charlotte,

My husband has just left me again for five months — let's see, that is September, October, November, December, and January — one, two, three, four, five months out of a year. You know, if you multiply those months by years, that could take a considerable heap out of your life together. As you already may have guessed, I'm writing to you on Sunday, and we (he) has just finished watching one football game, and another is ready to begin. We didn't even hear the Amen at Church this morning and barely had time for communion; the Cowboys were ready to kick off. I have read both papers, walked through the carpeted stadium several times, and would almost be ready to call his attorney and have his will probated, but occasionally his stare carries with it a blink of an eye, so he really isn't dead — just dead as far as I am concerned for five months.

With a wee bit of the devil in me, I decided when I fed him his lunch to test him — I put green cake coloring in the mashed potatoes, sprinkled the roast with pink coconut, put turnip greens on his plate (which he hates), and added purple coolaid to his milk, served it to him on a TV tray (what else? — the dining room table and breakfast table are as expendable as I for five months), and you know what? His eyes never moved. And as I crossed the sidelines of the stadium when he had finished his lunch to pick up the tray, he said, "Good lunch, honey, watch this instant replay."

And that's another thing. If I write to you on Sunday, there may be no more Dear Charlottes for 5 months, because of those cussed instant replays. If I've been knitting during the play, how can I pick up a stitch

during the instant replays? Yesterday for example, I was at my type-
writer, and it went like this —

Dear Cha
(Honey, come and watch the replay of this run).
Dear Charl
(Quick, they're going to rerun the field goal try).
Dear Charlot
(Can't you just sit down and watch? — look at that tackle on
the 20 yard line).

So, Charlotte, I guess I'll join him, and when I made those vows some 30
years ago that said, "wither thou goest," I darn sure didn't know that I'd
spend five months out of a year watching football!

Or I wouldn't have 'goest,'

B

I Wouldn't Trade You . . .

Dear Charlotte,

Darn it! Time does take its toll, and the wheels of the gods do grind slowly, but surely, and the grinding of those wheels has been too fast for me; and they (the wheels) have taken their toll.

In 1943 my husband told me, with prejudice, how pretty I was, how smart I was, how provocative I was, how irreplaceable I was, and that without me how his life would be a was —

In 1953 he told me what a wonderful mother I was, what a good housekeeper I was, what a good cook I was, what a good wife I was, and what a good manager I was —

In 1963 he told me what a good companion I was, what a good sounding board I was, what a good gardener and chauffeur I was, what a good doctor and nurse I was, what a good baby sitter I was, what a good lesson in patience I was, and what a good "Leave it to the Good Lord" example I was —

And now in September, 1973 — we were driving home — just the two of us from Dallas in a pouring rain. He was following a truck laden with watermelons, and certainly didn't find me pretty (no lipstick), provocative (too tired), wonderful (too selfish), or irreplaceable (too old), but as he was slowed down by the wet pavement and the truck (along with years), he slipped his hand in mine and spanned 30 years romantically with —

"Honey, I wouldn't trade you for a ripe load of watermelons."

It does take its toll,

B

Please Help Me

Dear Charlotte,

I pray that you will never have an LD child — or, on second thought, if you did, maybe you would understand. And you may or may not know that an LD child is a dear little boy or girl — mine or yours — with a learning disability. Experts tell us that 20 per cent of our children, even tho' they are very bright or average or below, are afflicted with a learning disability problem. That means, dear teacher or dear parent, that 6 children from a school room class of 30 face this problem — frightening? Yes, especially when one of these six belongs to you and when you hear her say —

"I am your child — please, help me — and, Mama, will you ask my teacher to help me, too?

Please ask my teacher to slow down and not talk too much like you do when you say, "Brush your teeth, comb your hair, make your bed, and pick up your pajamas" — all I seem to remember is "brush your teeth," and this gets me in trouble, and I get in real trouble at school when the teacher says, "Get out your paper, do problems 1 through 12, and write your name in the left hand corner." I just can't remember all the things I'm supposed to do, and I just sit —

And, too, Mama, do I always have to sit at the front of the school room or the very back, couldn't I just sit in the middle, so I wouldn't be different? 'Cause if I don't sit just in the middle, everyone knows I'm different. And when the teacher says she doesn't have time, does that mean me?

There are so many things I don't understand — why are there so many fours — like IV, or FOUR, or fore, and the number 4, and so many twos — like to, too, two, and just plain 2 — everyone else understands, but I don't — why, Mama, did God make so many fours and too many twos?

And I can't be still. Why do I have to sit at that hard desk that is too big for my feet to touch the floor and not say a word for so many hours? A big person could, but I can't. Why doesn't anyone care if my feet don't touch? Why could I move around where I wanted to in June and have to sit as quiet as a mouse in September? Tell me why — please help me.

And why, just why, does everything happen to me? I'm always the one who drops her pencil, or overturns the teacher's vase of flowers all over her papers, or can't find my nickels for milk, or spills my drink in the cafeteria — why is it always me? — why couldn't it sometimes happen to Peggy, or Jane, or Joe?

Peggy, Jane, or Joe won't play with me. Is it my fault? They don't seem to like me; I guess it's because I don't even like myself. And why does my teacher like Peggy, Jane, and Joe better than she likes me? Will you tell her to like me, too?

I'm your child, and I need help — do you like me? Why?"

Because I Love You,

Gusto!

Dear Charlotte,

On this late October Sunday, which is greyer than I, a TV commercial has just shattered the dismal day with, "You only get one time around in this old life, so live it with GUSTO!" Nodding in his battered, much-used recliner, my "for-better-or-worse" mate is catching a nap between halves of another football game! What am I doing? Taking an inventory of the GUSTO in our lives!

Let's see, once or twice a year we forget the clock and see the end of the Tonight show! GUSTO!

Each year we look forward to seeing Bert Parks and the Miss America pageant! That is really a GUSTOish Saturday night!

Our life had a terrific lift the year that we saw Patton and Airport in a real movie (not TV) — our first movies in 10 years — we were GUS-TOed with the language!

At 10 p.m. we often add GUSTO to our world with a glass of milk and chocolate puff cookies off the kitchen ledge.

We are travelers, too! We've been to Dallas this year, and I almost forgot, we drove to Tenaha and Timpson last week — with GUSTO!

We are spendthrifts with total abandonment! Last spring we purchased a lawn mower, two new garbage cans, and a clothesline, and two new tires for our car, which shows 80,000 miles of GUSTO!

We entertain lavishly, too — this year we had a slumber party, 2 weiner roasts, a birthday cake, and breakfast-on-the-floor during the Macy's parade!

Excuse me; the vibrant, much-alive male in our house has just awakened for the second half. He yawns, stretches, and has just said, "How about some buttered popcorn, honey? and to add a little GUSTO, bring me a Coke with an ice cream float!"

One time around!

B

Top of the Stove

Dear Charlotte,

I found it most difficult to be grateful for my many blessings last Thursday. I had to really talk to myself about gratitude, and it was all my husband's fault! Sometimes he isn't very bright! True, he has a University diploma hanging on the wall; he belongs to several professional organizations; he can decipher the stock market page each morning; he is a scholar of economics and chemistry, and he is so much wiser than I — most of the time. But —

Last Wednesday afternoon on Thanksgiving Eve, my stove oven quit and turned an ice-cold shoulder to me as I desperately begged it to work just one more day — to no avail! In answer to my tears and desperation, the "brain" of the house replied, "Don't panic, honey; just use the top of your stove tomorrow." TOP OF THE STOVE! I exploded. TOP OF THE STOVE? for turkey, sweet potato casserole, dressing, pumpkin pie, hot rolls? How could one, intelligent husband be so dumb?

Along with his high IQ, he believes that any call for help is an imposition. We visited with a friend Wednesday evening, who has a crew of electrical repairmen, and when this friend discovered my dilemma, he immediately and graciously offered help. "Oh, no," came from my wise mate, as he ignored the kick I administered to his shins under the table, "I(I?I?I?How about *me?*) wouldn't think of asking you to do this; it isn't important." (IT ISN'T IMPORTANT????)

Thanksgiving Day, as the learned head of our house watched 17 football games (or was it four?) from 10:00 A.M. to 11:00 P.M. (only 13 hours of football), I waited for friends to empty their ovens and spent the entire day carting and toting turkey, casseroles, etc., etc., etc., from my house to their house and from their house to my house.

When my beloved husband began the meal's blessing with "We are grateful for this Thanksgiving Day," I found it most difficult to say —

Amen,

B

What Is Thanksgiving?

Dear Charlotte,

It's a thankful day and a heart full of thanks day —
It's a cranberry and whipped cream day —
It's a homemade hot rolls and real butter day —
It's a high cost of living and wreck your budget day —
It's a giblet gravy on your tie day —
It's a Macy's parade and no cartoon day —
It's a white meat and gnaw on the turkey neck day —
It's an apple pie day, if you don't like pumpkin pie day —
It's a Texas Aggie or The University of Texas football day —
It's a mashed potato, creamed onions, or Yankee rutabaga day —
It's a white tablecloth and real napkin day —
It's a count your many blessings day —
It's a 'wish I had three ovens to my stove' day —
It's a Doxology and Our Father day —
It's a count the shopping days before Christmas day —
It's an out-of-school and no homework day —
It's a lean-back-in-your chair and houseshoe day —
It's a mountain of dishes and silver to wash day —
It's an indigestion and please hurry-to-bed day —
It's an appreciation of your neighbors, your friends, and your
    family day —
It's a love of God, your country, and your town day —
It's THANKSGIVING DAY!

Gratefully,

B

Smiling

Dear Charlotte,

Huge billboards dot our highways selling 'the real thing,' 'the UnCola,' 'the quiet ride,' 'the Thousandaire,' 'Happiness Is,' and many other products, which supposedly make our lives ones of comfort and joy.

Last week I was driving in a pouring rain when my windshield wipers suddenly refused to go another mile. They seemed tired — like me. Blessedly, I was close to a motor company, crept into the parking lot, and very efficiently locked my keys, purse, and umbrella safely inside the car as I slammed the door and stepped into the wet world.

A kind attendant came to my rescue, and I heard him mutter, "Stupid women," as he dug pine straw from the wipers and fished through glass and rubber with a coat hanger to extract my keys.

As I drove on to the highway with my old black suit soaked and limp, my Thursday hairdo a soggy, hairspray mess, and my spirits even blacker, 'limpier,' and 'soggier,' there loomed out of all the other problem-solving billboards — THIS one —

Smiling,
B

72

Needed!

Dear Charlotte,

Lately I have felt as needed and as obsolete as a Burma Shave sign or a pair of pointed toe shoes.

Any Mama needs to be needed —

Yesterday tho', dressed in my girdle best for a luncheon, an afternoon of bridge, and preparations made for six people for dinner, I all of a sudden became a physician, a pharmacist, a nurse, a cook, and a chauffeur, and a Mama. I accepted another collect call from Joe College Son and heard —

"Mama, I'm sick."

— I'm sorry, honey, how long have you been sick? —

"Four days, and I haven't eaten a thing. Maybe I could eat a little bit of your potato soup; I might keep it down."

— Do you have any fever? —

"I don't know; I broke the thermometer in my mouth. Is mercury dangerous?"

— Have you called a doctor? —

"No, I lost the name and phone number of the one Daddy gave me, and I couldn't pay him anyway, 'cause I can't find my check book. Did I leave it at home?"

— Have you taken any medicine? —

"No, I gave it to my roommate. He had appendicitis."

— ?!?!?!?!????? — Where do you hurt? —

"All over, remember how sick I was with the red measles?"

— Tell me what you want me to do, son —

"Can I come home, Mama, and can you come and get me?"

— Can I come and get you? LIKE YESTERDAY — I'm on my way —

NEEDED,

B

An Old Friend

Dear Charlotte,

I said goodby to an old friend a few weeks ago — the friend was my 19 year old stove. The tired, old stove was the age of my son — he, and it, sorta became close to my heart during those years.

Of course, my astute husband swore that I didn't take very good care of the enameled 19 year old, or it wouldn't have had such an early demise. Let's see — with just my faulty arithmetic, I can give that outdated, greasy old friend credit for 18,000 hamburgers, 52,000 pancakes, 800 roasts, 20,000 eggs, 40,000 pieces of bacon, 100,000 pieces of toast, 2,000 chickens, 400 turkeys — not to mention gallons and gallons of egg custard, which happens to be you-know-who's favorite dessert!

I agree that the oven wouldn't bake the best angel food cake in the world — the spring was sprung on the oven door — and there was always a tiny space between stove and door. However, if I wanted a good cake, I could lean against the door for 30 or 45 minutes, and suffer only minor burns. The door wasn't my fault — the children were to blame — they weighed too much. On winter mornings they perched on the door, sipped "coffee milk" while the oven took the chill off the kitchen and them. Warm children — or fluffy angel food?

As my old friend was carried out the back door, Its four black eyes seemed to say to me, "How could you? You chipped my shiny, white face by warming baby bottles at 2:00 a.m. — by pushing an iron skillet back and forth while corn popped — by letting French fry grease catch on fire — you'll miss me."

And I do,

B

A Heap of Living

Dear Charlotte,

My apologies to Edgar A. Guest —

It takes a heap of living in a house to make it home,
Send your ten year old daughter off to boarding school,
And you will feel that your world is gone.
You'll really appreciate the things she left behind,
And hurt to touch her, and she's always on your mind.
It doesn't make any difference how happy you try to be,
Home ain't home without her for her Dad and me.

Home is a place where you're busy every minute.
Before it's home, there's got to be some children living in it.
Within the walls there's got to be a lot of noise, and then
When they are gone, the quiet echoes over and over again.

The heap of living is a mixture of so many things —
Like pink lemonade glasses on the kitchen ledge,
And playhouses built under the hedge,
A room as cluttered as it can be,
And a rope swing in a tree,
Smudges and fingerprints on every door,
And muddy sneakers to mark the floor.
You've got to set an extra plate or two for lunch,
And count the chicken pieces when there's a bunch.
You've got to search for socks and your personal comb —
It takes a heap of living in a house to make it home.

You've got to sweep to make it home, and sit and sigh
At the ironing board and dirty clothes piled high.
And in the stillness of the night, you've got to hit the floor
To be sure they're warm and that you've locked the back door.
You find that home is dearer with a child
Even tho' they often drive you wild
With their tugging at you always, and you never have a minute,
Before it's home, you've got to do some living in it.

You've got to have children to sing and dance and play,
And love them for keeping you busy each day.
You've got to watch them grow year by year,
And know they're a part of you —
Oh, how dear!
You've got to send a child to school and turn 'n say g'bye,
And just sorta pretend you've got something in your eye.
You've got to count the days and hours she's been away,
And wait for the postman and visitation day.

You've got to hear the quiet that she's left behind,
And pick up all the little things you find —
Her books, her toys, her shoes, her treasures
Before you really realize the countless pleasures
That your child really does impart —
A home without a child is a house without a heart.

But you've also got to know when school is over, and she is back
For summer vacation; at times a suitcase you'd gladly pack
For her, or yourself, so you'd have peace and be alone —
It sure takes a heap of living in a house to make it home.

"Is There a Santa Claus, Mama?"

Dear Charlotte,

The age-old question came from my 8 year old this week — "Mama, my friends tell me there is no Santa Claus; is there, Mama; is there?"

There must be no more difficult question for a parent. My answer, with tears in my voice, went like this —

"Yes, dear, there is a Santa Claus; there will always be a Santa Claus. When you grow up and become a woman and have a child of your own, you will answer, "Yes, my dear, there is a Santa Claus.

Santa Claus will live in your heart forever as long as there is —

A butterfly, spring flowers, runny noses, a swing in a tree, dirty fingernails, a Christmas carol that says 'Silent Night,' peanut butter sandwiches, popsicles, bubble gum, ice cream cones, fire trucks, 2 plus 2 equals 4, school bells, storybooks, hair ribbons, candles on a birthday cake, presents wrapped with ribbon, brothers that yell at you, mothers that wash blankets when you've been sick, fathers that love you, grape jelly, Cokes, 18 crayolas, Charlie Brown, Go-Go boots, warm baths, your blue blanket, a dog who sleeps by your bed, cartoons on Saturday, Dr. Bird, Church on Sunday, a flag on the Fourth of July, swimming pools, picnics, your swing set, wagons, dolls, bicycles, a red apple, a tangerine, mixed nuts, your Easter basket, your favorite T shirt, the lonely child in your room, the sick lady in the next block, our neighbor who is old, your red houseshoes, the warm kitchen when you're cold, a hug when you have been good, a Band-Aid when you've skinned your knee, a star on a tree, and the story of a baby in a manger —

Yes, dear, there is a Santa Claus, and there always will be —"

Peace on Earth?

Dear Charlotte,

For almost six years now we have sent a family picture on our Christmas card, and six years ago our daughter was a cuddly two months old baby — our son, an amiable, willing 8 year old with a neat crew cut. Each year it has grown (along with Bill, Jr.'s, hair) more difficult to make this picture. I really wouldn't try so hard, except our friends expect a perfect family scene. But last Sunday afternoon, I was adamant in saying, "This is the end — never again!"

Immediately after Church, with dishes in the sink, beds unmade, bathrooms holy bedlam, I begged a dear friend and neighbor to come and take our Christmas card picture of family bliss!

As she arrived, the grumbles began — Daddy: "Aw, honey, not now; did you know that Navy beat Army, and I haven't even seen the sport page?" Bill, Jr.: "Mother, for Pete sakes, I'm too old to do this; where's my sweat shirt?" (which reads, Love me or Leave me — I'm a dropout!!) Betty Ann: "I won't do it; I want to play with Janetta Ruth; where's my toast with grape jelly on it? I don't like this white dress. Where are my tennis shoes?"

The first pose was taken in the living room, (only room not in disarray). Bill, Jr., decided to yank his sister's hair to keep her still. All heck broke loose with tears, yells, and mother's exasperation —

Second pose (in dining room) Betty Ann discovered that she had a sticker in the seat of her new leotards — brother was disgusted; daddy was amused, and mother was close to explosion —

Third pose — Daddy decided that the flashbulbs weren't working properly and delivered a lecture on efficiency and being prepared, as Betty Ann dashed to the bathroom —

Fourth pose — maybe, just maybe the children will look angelic, daddy's head won't be cut off, and mother's gritted teeth will look like a genuine smile,

And then the caption will read,

"Peace on earth — from our house to yours."

I'm Dreaming

Dear Charlotte,

I'm dreaming of a no-football Christmas,
Just like the ones I used to know,
When my husband's eyes glistened, and he didn't frown,
'Cause the Cowboys fumbled on the very first down!

I'm dreaming of a long ago Christmas Day,
When I didn't have to catch each instant replay,
When we used to welcome guests as they rang the doorbell,
And we didn't share Christmas with Howard Cosell.

I'm dreaming of a Christmas that I can be with Bill
And not compete with Calvin Hill.
Long for those days when we never differed,
And our moments weren't invaded with Frank Gifford.

Won't the football sponsors be a wee bit merciful?
You can't celebrate Christmas during a commercial.
To each of them I dedicate this missal
Don't shatter this Day with a referee's whistle.

I'm dreaming of Christmas with memories fond
Without the homespun humor of "Dandy Don" —
Couldn't we keep Christmas in an old-fashioned manner?
And sing Silent Night instead of the Star Spangled Banner?

I find it difficult to be merry, and I frown instead of laugh
When I have to serve my Christmas dinner during the half.
I'm dreaming, just dreaming, but please let it be.
Please, can't we have Christmas without the TV?

B

He Was Different

Dear Charlotte,

Last night beside a warm fire my child and I curled up on the couch and watched "Rudolph, the Red-Nosed Reindeer." It was a beautiful, new version of this story, or else, I had never bothered to really listen to its heart-catching message.

You see, Rudolph was a deer misfit — not a people misfit — but a misfit, nonetheless. He had a physical handicap — the heart-breaking handicap of a shiny, red, bulbous nose, which embarrassingly glowed and glowed. And to the staid, stilted society of reindeers, Rudolph's abnormality made him totally unacceptable to them, and of course, they passed their views on to their children.

Rudolph's peers wouldn't let him join their reindeer games; the adult deers were filled with derision and revulsion, and even Rudolph's parents were ashamed of their little deer, because he did not fit their deer world; he was different.

Different, yes, but he possessed many qualities which the big or little deers didn't have. He was kind, lovable, generous, compassionate, and humble (which most deers aren't). He begged his deer world for affection, acceptance, and approval, but his world could not see beyond Rudolph's nose (or their's).

He did find a friend tho' — another misfit — a little elf who didn't want to be an elf. This misfit elf wanted to be a dentist, but this was taboo; the adult elves and their children insisted that he had to be an elf. So, Rudolph and the molar-loving elf sought another world and found a world of misfits — a doll who couldn't walk, wet, or say 'Mama,' a toy locomotive with square wheels, a Jack-in-the-box who had been banished because his name was Charlie-in-the-box, and a water gun that shot jelly instead of water. These misfits accepted Rudolph — nose and all —

You know the ending of the story. One foggy Christmas Eve Santa Claus decided to cancel Christmas, because he had no one to guide his sleigh through the stormy night. And then like a miracle, Rudolph with his glowing nose was chosen for this glorious task. No longer was Rudolph a misfit; he was needed; he had been given the most wonderful Christmas gifts of all —

The Night Before Christmas

Dear Charlotte,

'Twas the night before Christmas, and all through the house
Everybody was stirring except my dear spouse.
All had been wrapped, polished, and done (including me),
And I felt like a dead partridge on a low limb of a pear tree.
The children weren't even close to their beds —
As television and Beatle records blared through their heads.

Daddy had settled in his chair for a well-deserved nap.
Golf Magazine and TV Guide had slipped to his lap.
When out in the den, there arose such a clatter,
I sprang from the dish water to see what was the matter.
The Christmas tree was falling and leaning toward town
And at any moment would come crashing down.

"Let me open a present, Mama; please just one —
You never let me have any fun."
"May I go to the Top Burger?" came from the other.
"I don't like ham and turkey; please, can't I, Mother?"
"And something's burning; it must be the pie,
And I forgot to wrap Daddy's new tie."
The smoke from the kitchen circled my head like a wreath,
As Santa roused from his chair and shouted, "Good grief!
What's all this hustle and bustle and noise?
Get the children to bed and give me the toys.

Did you get Betty Ann her new bike and Bill a new ski?
I do wish you could be as efficient as me.
I know I told you in November that the budget was slim,
But you know we have just one her and one him —

Why can't you relax; you've nothing to do —
Parents have done this for years; it isn't very new,
I hope you don't have anything that must be put together.
I'm so sleepy; it just must be the weather."
With a wink of his eye and a twist of his head
I knew right away he was headed for bed.

As I turned off the light and locked the back door,
A question came to me that I could not ignore —
"Is it all worth it?" I wanted to sing.
"It's Christmas," came back, "and would you change a thing?"
"Not one thing," I whispered, "when they are all out of sight.
MERRY CHRISTMAS to all, and to all a Good Night."